OLD EXETER

A Classic Collection of Archive Photographs relating to the City of Exeter

From Victorian Times to approximately 1940

by

Peter Thomas

THE ISCA COLLECTION

The Isca Collection was first started in 1974 by the author after the discovery that a huge collection of photographic plates and negatives were liable to be disposed of. The resource was the work of Mr Henry Wykes and his assistant Marjorie Hockmuth. Following the closure of the "Wykes Studio" in Northernhay Place, Exeter, in 1974, the author was to obtain the complete collection of some 42,000 half-plate negatives. Examination of these records showed Exeter as it had been since around 1910 up to 1970. It was obvious that the work was of vital importance to the history of Exeter and started the author's passion for collecting photographic records of the City of Exeter. To date the collection includes negatives, prints, slides, albums, books and other items of interest.

In the following years numerous exhibitions have been undertaken, assistance given with TV documentaries relating to Exeter, Radio interviews and press coverage. The collection has been responsible for a number of publications to date including "Old Exeter", "Aspects of Exeter" (co-author Jacqueline Warren),"The House That Moved," "Exeter in Old Postcards," "Exeter in Old Photographs". It has assisted with illustrations for a variety of publications. The Collection is the largest private collection of Exeter records and is recorded with The Royal Photographic Society in the British Photographic Record, a directory of historical photographic Collections.

ABOUT THE AUTHOR

Exonian, Peter Thomas has lived and worked all his life in his native City of Exeter. He was born in 1948. He attended Holloway Street School, Central School and Episcopal School for boys. The first and last schools have now changed roles and Central School has been demolished.

From an early age he acquired an interest in photography, encouraged by his god-mother. She lectured extensively throughout the County using "Kodachrome" slides, a very new concept at the time, and also an unusual occupation for a woman.

At the age of 15 the author started work in the building trade and used his photographic talents to record his company's work relating to the restoration of Devon's churches. He then joined the photographic retail trade.

As a self taught photographer his main interest has revolved around natural history, however he has diversified considerably. He has specialised in the history of photography and the author amassed a considerable collection of historical photographic equipment and images. Numerous lectures have been given on this subject.

In 1974 he formed "The Isca Collection", a collection of historical photographic images relating to Exeter. A great deal of time has been spent acquiring images for the Collection. It is the largest private collection in existence to the author's knowledge. Also specialising on the photographic history of Exeter the author has given many lectures over the years and appeared on television, radio and gained publicity in newspapers.

A reputation has been acquired as a local author with the production of the books "Old Exeter", Aspects of Exeter", "The House That Moved", Exeter in Old Postcards", "The Exe Estuary (Wildlife in camera)" and "Exeter in Old Photographs". He has supplied numerous illustrations for other publications. Photographs have been accepted by HRH Queen Elizabeth, the Queen Mother, the late Sir Peter Scott, Lord Clinton and the book "Aspects of Exeter" was received by HRH Prince Charles, Prince of Wales.

The author has travelled extensively and taken an interest in the work of the World Wide Fund for Nature. An extensive trip was taken to Mexico, El Salvador and Australia.

His current position is that of Tourism Promotion and Support Officer for Exeter City Council.

CONTENTS

LIST OF PLATES

INTRODUCTION

The main purpose of this book is to provide a unique visual record of the County Town of Devon, as it was until approximately 1940. The City of Exeter has one of the most impressive documented histories of any City or town in the country but its visual history has been somewhat overlooked. Hopefully this book and any others that may come after will provide the Exeter resident and many of our visitors with an unparalleled resource which will prove valuable not only historically but also from the point of view of education.

The majority of the young people in Exeter will be totally unaware of the scenes that appear throughout this book and in this age of environmental awareness it is perhaps more essential that they understand how our own City has progressed through the ages. By viewing these archive records they will have a greater appreciation of the kind of City their parents, grandparents and great grandparents grew up in. It will I hope give them inspiration to enquire, question and understand Exeter and its past. I am hopeful that those working in education will grasp this chance to utilise these records for the benefit of their pupils and that it will assist them in stimulating the interest of Exeter's children.

As the pages of this book are turned many people will be viewing a City which will in many ways be unfamiliar to them for as with many places, Exeter has changed beyond recognition in comparison to its prewar character.

It is this very fact which I am seeking to record in the form of permanent publications which will be a ready visual reference for anyone interested in discovering the changing face of Exeter.

These records of Exeter are classic studies which show the City as it had been for many years and will give the reader a tour through the old streets from the River Exe to the end of Blackboy Road, and out into Devon's countryside by coach and horses. I have been careful in the selection of photographs to give as wide a coverage as possible but also presenting some of the finest and most interesting records from The Isca Collection.

The average size of negative has been half-plate ($6\frac{1}{2} \times 4\frac{3}{4}$) therefore the detail obtained is unsurpassed in quality. All have been handprinted. It was not until 1826 that the first permanent photographic image was obtained and within a period of 150 years phenomenal developments have taken place with photography. The vast majority of these photographs were taken with plate cameras, either wooden or metal, which meant quite an effort carrying all the equipment around. The results however would stand against any work done today. In the earlier years of photography the photographer would have had his own studio, usually in a prominent position within the town or City and would undertake all manner of work. By the end of his working life often a tremendous archive would have been established — a unique resource. It has not been unusual for such studio collections to be sent to the tip, with the result that irreplaceable records have been lost for good. Today these collections are proving to be priceless for many people studying local history, undertaking research or those who want to recreate, restore or revitalise buildings and areas which have disappeared.

The bombing of Exeter in 1942 was to change the City in a way which had never been achieved in the whole of its history. It was however not just the actual war damage itself but the following irradication of many of the City's more historic areas that changed its character to its present image. The visitor to Exeter would however be quite unaware of these dramatic and often controversial changes. The sight of records such as these often result in the people's sheer amazement that local destruction of such proportions have taken place in such an historic City such as Exeter.

Many of us have short memories and with the pace of life today it is no wonder that we cannot recall just how things were. Having such scenes reduced onto a page also brings other things to our attention such as the variety, scale and architecture of buildings in a street. Above all it creates a talking point where father will relate to son, grandfather to grandson and so on, in this way preserving our knowledge and interest in the subject. Certainly with books of this nature it is a vital ingredient and has over the years brought many interesting aspects to my attention, thanks to readers.

As an Exonian I have often been totally absorbed by a photograph, trying to discover where it was and why it was taken. People have often asked me "How on earth did you know that? You were not even born." The forming of the Isca Collection has given me a most valauble insight as to what Exeter was like before its radical changes and today I can still enthuse in the same way. Over the years I have had many approaches to assist with projects, talks on Exeter, and to produce books on the City. There is no doubt in my mind that today there is more genuine interest in the history of Exeter than there has ever been. Public opinion is strong for the retention of historic buildings and sites and people are not slow at coming forward to voice their opinions. It is important that we retain the best of our heritage in whatever form it may be. It is only appropriate therefore that the work of such photographers is available for the benefit of all.

P Thomas
Abbey Road
Exeter
1990

Plate 1   Aerial View of Exeter (c1927)

This excellent record of Exeter was taken by Mr Henry Wykes around 1927. Henry Wykes died at the age of 90 and it was said that he was the oldest aerial photographer in the country at the time.

Looking from the the bottom of the photograph to the right is a line of white buildings. This is South Street which prewar was far narrower than it is today. There are few records of old South Street. At the top of the road is a large building. This was Lloyds Cigarette Factory. Clearly shown standing in front of the Cathedral is St Mary Majors Church. This was demolished in 1971.

The Cathedral Close is shown containing many mature English Elms. These were later to be lost totally due to Dutch Elm Disease.

"Mols Coffee House" is seen in the corner of The Close.

At this time the High Street runs from South Street to Sidwell Street maintaining its original width. After the post war rebuilding this was to be altered. Halfway up the High Street can be seen another line of white buildings. This was Queen Street before the demolition of those buildings. The whole of the opposite corner and a substantial area of buildings were to be demolished in the post war period. The central area of the photograph is dominated not only by the Cathedral but by Bedford Circus which stands behind. The narrow entrance from Bedford Street to High Street can be seen. Behind the Circus is the school and playground of St Johns School. Southernhay is seen right behind Bedford Circus with its fine houses flanking each side. The Southernhay Congregational Church stands dominating the area.

At the top of High Street and joining Sidwell Street is the London Inn Square. Much of the area beyond has since disappeared since this record was taken.

THE EXE BRIDGES

Exeter owes it's location and importance to the fact that it is situated on the last suitable place for crossing the river Exe at its seaward end. Until 1231 the only means of crossing the river was by ferry boat or a very narrow wooden bridge which would only take the weight of a human being. There was also a ford, where people frequently lost their lives trying to get into the City. They were often swept into the river.

The first proper bridge of stone with 18 magnificent arches was built thanks to Walter Gervase, Mayor of Exeter. The foundations were laid in 1257. Through the passage of time it was repaired and improved, but eventually traffic was too congested and a new bridge was built by 1778. A three arched bridge this time as seen in our next photograph. The cost of building was £30,000. At first there were problems with construction, but after the foundations were laid on solid rock no more problems arose. It is interesting to note the first vehicle to cross the bridge was a hearse!

With the coming of the tram it was again necessary to replace the old bridge with a new structure. Made in iron, a single span bridge was opened in 1905 by the Mayor C. Perry. To maintain access during construction a wooden pontoon bridge was situated beside the stone bridge. It was dismantled after the construction was completed. Alas, the iron bridge has now disappeared and has been replaced by concrete structures. A bonus derived from this and the revised schemes is the exposure of the remains of the old medieval stone bridge.

It is most fortunate that we have some excellent records of the old stone bridge, the new iron bridge, its construction and the opening ceremony. These have been reproduced from some fine 12×10 glass plates that are still in existence.

Plate 2 **The three arched stone Exe Bridge completed 1778 (c1900)**

s particular scene showing the three arched stone bridge spanning the River Exe gives a feeling of quietness, a more tranquil way of life and a river
quietly flowed by old Exeter. Taken around 1890 it was not to be long before this scene was to be eradicated by a new structure in 1905.
Fundamental changes were to take place in the riverside areas which would change its character as never before.

Plate 3 The frozen River Exe (c1890)

A fascinating record taken from the north side of the stone Exe Bridge looking towards St Thomas. This scene obviously caused a great deal of interest. There are records of severe winters where the River Exe has frozen so hard that Oxen have been roasted on it. This could have been quite feasible as at one time the river was far shallower than it is today.

Plate 4   Ice Yacht on the River Exe (c1870)

rare to get such interesting early photographs as it shows locals having fun with a home made ice yacht on the River Exe. This particular photograph
found quite by chance pinned to the darkroom door of the Exeter photographer Henry Wykes. The original, in poor condition was shown with a
y done by Wykes to show how old photos could be restored.

Plate 5 **Construction of the new iron Exe Bridge 1904**

In 1903 the old stone bridge was demolished and was to be replaced with this single span iron bridge. The new bridge being wider was to ea
accommodate the new electric trams. A new era had started for Exeter's riverside. Note the barges used for transporting materials for construction
the new bridge. In the background can be seen the tower of St Edmunds church with the City Brewery in front of it. The tower marks the line of the
medieval bridge of which a substantial portion still remained under the road surface. Nearly 70 years later the bridge portions were to be excavated a
restored, and today stand in a landscaped area. The remains of this ancient bridge has been declared a National Monument.

Plate 6   Removal of pontoon bridge prior to opening of Exe Bridge 1905

s excellent record shows the dismantling of the temporary wooden bridge which was used during the construction of the new iron bridge. ctators are seen looking over the bridge at the workmen undertaking the work. In the centre of the new bridge suspended on planks is a painter ting the finishing touches before the official opening ceremony. The view looks towards St Thomas and in the background can be seen the station ch at the time was covered. All the relevant buildings shown have been demolished in the post war years.

***Plate* 7   The new Exe Bridge looking to St Thomas 1905**

Plate 8 **The opening Ceremony Exe Bridge 29th March 1905**

Mayor C Perry is seen surrounded by dignitaries who have gathered on the Bridge

Plate 9   **Opening ceremony on Exe Bridge showing ceremonial rope (1905)**

This was to be one of the grandest opening ceremonies the City had ever seen. Hundreds of people flocked to the riverside to gaze at this masterpiece of engineering. Mayor C Perry declared the bridge open and cut a rope which stretched from one side of the bridge to the other. A ce section of the rope complete with a label was given to the author some years ago. The label reads "Rope used for opening of Exe Bridge 1905". It found tucked behind some old attic beams in Blackboy Road.

Plate 10 **The opening of the new Alphington Road extension for Electric trams 1906**

or C Perry is seen crossing over Exe Bridge on the way to Alphington Road. The tram clearly shows the destination of the new route. This
ed to be another popular event for Exonians. Control was kept by a policeman holding an umbrella!

Plate 11   **Looking from Cowick Street to New Bridge Street across Exe Bridge (c1910)**

Plate 12 **The River Exe showing Gervase Avenue and Exe Bridge (c1910)**

building of the new Exe Bridge also brought with it changes to the immediate areas adjacent to the new structure. A new riverside path was
ed and the riverside flanked by ornate railings. A number of buildings were removed to enable this to take place. The edges of the River Exe
starting to be controlled.

Plate 13   **Skating on the frozen River Exe (c1914)**

Plate 14   The Quay

The Quay at Exeter has been the vital link which led to the city's wealth. It was from the Port of Exeter that large quantities of woollen cloth were exported in times gone by. Goods were also imported via the Quay directly into the City. The link between the Quay and the estuary was the Exeter Canal, the oldest Pound Lock Canal in England. The two warehouses shown were built in 1835. With the advent of the railway in 1844 the Quay found it difficult to compete with the new service of rail and by the turn of the twentieth century the port was in a steep decline. Today the whole area of the Quay and riverside has been subject to a massive transformation programme of development and tourism promotion.

Plate 15   **Shipping at the Quay (c1880)**

Plate 16   **St Leonard's Quay (c1880)**

area which stands at the bottom of Quay Hill was known as St Leonard's Quay. It was here that vessels used to tie up and take ballast on board. often this would be in the form of scrap metal. The few records that exist often show large piles of industrial scrap alongside the Quay waiting to be taken on board.

Plate 17   "The Basin" or "Wet Dock" by Bedford (c1870)

This photograph taken by the photographer "Bedford" shows the Basin or Wet Dock around 1870. Cut elm trees line the sides of the Basin. Forme[r]ly the head of the Canal, The Basin, was opened on the 29th September 1830. Barges with streamers took large groups of people down to the Do[ck] Locks and back. After the grand opening ceremony a sumptuous dinner was given by the Chamber of Trade.

Plate 18 **The Canal Inspection (c1880)**

...er City Council are responsible for the maintenance of the Exeter Canal which is the oldest Pound Lock Canal in England. It was customary for the ...ncil to inspect the Canal on a yearly basis to ensure its up keep. Here a concerned group of Councillors undertake their duties on behalf of the City ...nd 1880.

27

Plate 19   **The opening of the Port Royal 1904**

Plate 20   Steam tug towing on the Canal (c1890)

as customary to use horses for the towing of ships on the canal. There were different staging posts for the animals along the canal. Care had to be n as sometimes the horses would slip and fall into the Canal. Records show that animals were sometimes drowned whilst carrying out such ities.

Steam tugs were also used for towing purposes as shown in this record.

Plate 22   Shepherd driving sheep to Bonhay Road Market (c1900)

lightful record of a shepherd driving his sheep along Bonhay Road to Market. On the right hand side is the premises of Messrs Parkins who
alise in iron and steel products. This included the making of horse shoes.

Plate 21   "The Star and Garter" Public House (c1930)

building stood on the corner of Bonhay Road just after leaving Exe Bridge. The old cattle market operated behind the building for many years and
situated at the water's edge on Bonhay Road.
This was typical of the older Exeter pubs and probably attracted many farming folk.

Plate 23
Shepherd at the market
(c1900)

A classic study of a Devon shep[herd]
complete with bowler hat at [the]
Bonhay Road Cattle Market. It w[ould]
not be unusual for shepherds to [walk]
their flocks a number of miles [to]
Exeter for the sales. Even [now]
Exeter is of prime importance fo[r the]
farming industry.

Plate 24   The selling of council horses Bonhay Road Market

Bonhay Road Market was to mark the end of an era when the Council horses were sold. Today with the proliferation of motor cars it is difficult to imagine that life proceeded at a horses pace. Refuse would be collected by these delightful animals who had wicker baskets strapped on them.

Plate 25 **The Higher Leat showing Leat Terrace**

Many centuries ago waterways or "Leats" were constructed to operate the city's mills. The source of water was taken from the River Exe and was extracted at Head Weir Mills. The leats although drastically altered still exist today. The Higher Leat is shown here at Leat Terrace, a delightful row of cottages which were only very recently demolished. Behind is seen Tremletts Tannery which was opposite St Edmunds Church. The leat still runs today and is a fundamental part of a new development scheme.

HAM'S NOTED WHISKY

MINERAL WATERS BEST QUALITY

C.HAM FOR WHISKY ESTABLISHED 1829.

Exeter. Fore Street.

Plate 26   Fore Street (c1910)

e Street Hill has traditionally attracted many of Exeter's tradesmen and was also the main shopping area for the people of the West Quarter. The
et still contains a wide variety of businesses and many of its older buildings are being refurbished. The steepness of the street caused problems for
ses and trams alike and accidents were not uncommon.

35

Plate 27   Traction Engine accident Fore Street 1906

On the 25th of April 1906 the shop of Walter Ottons had a slight surprise when a traction engine carrying a large load of bricks crashed outside. S
were the perils of Fore Street.

Plate 28   Tram crash at Exe Bridge 1917

...record shows the famous tram crash which ended in disaster on Exe Bridge. The vehicle had got out of control on Fore Street Hill and hurtled ...ards Exe Bridge where finally it overturned. Unfortunately lives were lost. The scene was captured by the photographer Henry Wykes who quickly ...cessed his plates and within one hour was selling postcards of the event outside his Studio at Exe Bridge. Note the covered body.

WEST GATE

Coming from Fore Street down West Street we enter the West Quarter. Originally, the old West Gate of the City stood opposite the charming little church of St Mary Steps. Unfortunately the Gate was removed in 1814. The whole of this area was chiefly inhabited by fullers, dyers, weavers and other trades needing proximity to water. Previously wealthy merchants had resided in this area, but with increasing fortune moved to larger houses.

Many of the old houses were converted to other uses. Today we are fortunate there still remains a most charming part of this quarter, much of which has been renovated.

During the period illustrated on the following pages you see glimpses of the poverty that existed in the West Quarter.

The famous "Matthew The Miller" church clock shows the four seasons. The centre statue is said to be Henry VIII and it bends forward on the hour. On each side of Henry stands a soldier, both hold a javelin and a hammer with which they alternately strike the quarter hours. The name "Matthew The Miller" is derived from an old miller who was noted for his punctuality in visiting his customers at certain hours of the day.

Plate 29   West Street (c1910)

Plate 30 (opposite)
ary Steps Church and 24 West Street

ancient building shown left was to be
blished in the early 1930's leaving a
antial area which adjoined the City Wall at the
f the old West Gate to the City. The building
would certainly have been classified as that
Historic Interest". Over 30 years later another
ing of similar nature was to be deposited on
ite after being removed from the corner of
Street. Today that building is simply known as
House That Moved". This single event
ed world-wide news.

Plate 31
The clock "Matthew The Miller"

This fascinating clock has been a major attraction
of the West Quarter and still has a great many
visitors to gaze up at it. Another local tale is that it
was put up in memory of a miller who so regular in
his habits that all the local community could time
their day by his movements. Upon his death they
collected sufficient funds to have the clock put up
in his memory.

Plate 32   **West Street (c1900)**

tionally the West Quarter has held a great
nation for artists. The area at one time a home
wealthy merchants acquired a number of
rtant and attractive buildings. By the end of
0th century the area had become the City's
r slum problem. In the 1930's the West
ter was subject to a radical demolition
ramme with its residents being rehoused in
developments. Today little is left of what was
f the City's most historic areas.

Plate 33   **Stepcote Hill (c1900)**

Plate 34   Family at Stepcote Hill
                (c1890)

ecords of working people perhaps show us
about the state of society than anything else.
tiny alley which appears to have no name
the rear of St Mary Steps Church. The father
s recorded with what appears to be a large
! Note the ghost image of the boy in the
round.

Plate 35   Stepcote Hill

Exeter's most famous Street was the main entry into the City from the west. At one
time referred to as "Mule Steps Way". It is clearly shown that the children would often
play in the central section which was an open gutter.

Plate 3
West Stree
Stepcote

Plate 37
Frog Street (c1900)

n archive illustration of the
er that has passed there
d be little to compare with
study of Frog Street. The
e of this street was to be
olished with the construc-
of Western Way, the new
system which came down
across the River Exe. The
se on the left was to be
oved in 1961 to the site in
Street adjacent to where the
West Gate had stood. Here it
en in a reasonable state,
h was not the case on its
oval.

Plate 38   The Tudor House
(c1920)

Another property situated this time o[...]
Island which was to become in a ru[...]
state before it was rescued. Dating from [...]
thought, the 17th century this propert[...]
bought by an individual in the mid 1[...]
and totally restored. Believed to have [...]
originally a merchants house the scal[...]
slate front bears Coats of Arms. The [...]
slate work shown once covered the [...]
upper front but is said to have [...]
destroyed in the 1820's

Plate 39 (opposite)
Tudor Street families (c1900[...]

The visit of the photographer causes [...]
excitement as this is a rare treat for [...]
families. The result of 12 years painsta[...]
restoration, without using any mo[...]
means, the house today stands as a tribu[...]
its restorer, Mr Bill Lovell. It is at pr[...]
a restaurant.

48

TUCKERS HALL

Containing one of the most delightful rooms in Exeter and situated inconspicuously in the centre of Fore Street, "Tuckers Hall" is often missed by the passer-by. The hall dates from 1471 and belongs to the Company of Weavers, Fullers and Shearmen, the last of Exeter's ancient Guilds which was created in 1490. The room is the same today as when this photograph was taken, and shows one of the finest examples of an oak panelled chamber that exists in England.

The hall is still used today on limited occasions by members and privileged guests. Being directly connected with the woollen industry we can see illustrated early tillet blocks used for marking the bales of wool. To outline their history. an extract from an article in The Western Antiquary of July 1882, written by Mr. Harry Hems of Exeter.

JULY, 1882. THE WESTERN ANTIQUARY.

Note on the Illustrations.
FOUR OLD TILLET BLOCKS.

In the last century Exeter had, next to Leeds, the largest woollen market in the Kingdom. The trade had long been connected with the former ancient city, and Parliamentary records of the beginning of the 16th century woollen goods from Exeter are frequently mentioned. At the commencement of the 18th century, it is sa the trade was so general, that eight out of every ten citizens were connected with it. In 1750 over 300,000 pieces of woollen goods, valued at a million pounds exported from Exeter, yet if we except the ancient Hall of the Tuckers, Weavers, and Shearmen and their Charities, we have little or nothing now to remind us of a trade which has altogether passed away from our midst.

The four illustrations which appear in this issue, are actual prints from as many wooden blocks, which were at one time, actively connected with Exeter's staple They are the trade marks of old merchants of the 18th century, and were used as distinguishing devices stamped upon bales of woollen goods—The cloth for expor was wrapped in pieces of buckram—called "tillets"—and these stamps were known as tillet blocks. The making of the blocks was a speciality, and there is a character the few that yet remain, which goes to prove, that in spite of the non-existence of schools of art in those days, the art workman knew how to make bold, good lines, s as they were in composition, but full of effect and power. My esteemed friend, Mr. George Townsend, the accomplished antiquarian of Exeter, has some interesting in his possession, and there are five examples in the Albert Museum at Exeter. These were a gift to the city by Mr. T. B. Davey. a citizen of renown, who is a decend

the old tillet printers. They are all precisely the size of these illustrated, one represents 3 lions rampant, with a moth upon a raised ribbon beneath; another has the letters G. R. under an elongated cross; a third represents a man working at a loom; the fourth has a full face in a sun, whilst below the letters A R and the mongram NP. are inclosed within a heart; the fifth has a lion rampant like unto the one now shown. This block, however, is set into a much larger one, whichconsists of mantling of a very ornate character, surmounted by a Tudor rose, and is altogether nearly two feet square. The four portrayed in the accompanying issue are in my own collection. I acquired them, some years ago, of an elderly lady, who had had them in her possession ever since she could remember.

It seems that the trade mark was first put on the wraps in a showy colour by means of a stencil, and ultimately completed by the impression of the tillet block. This was printed on by a tillet press. Afterwards when disused for this purpose, the old presses got adapted for ordinary type printing.

And this latter observation suggests the remark that the art of stamping impressions in this manner, and of producing representations of religious subjects by wood blocks was very probably the original suggestor of the whole art and mystery of printing.

The ups and downs of life are illustrated in these curious tillet blocks the trade and the traders have gone; and these, the "trade-marks" of the western merchants, are now of no monetary, but of historic value. In Yorkshire and other parts of England, where manufacturers not only "strive, but thrive," a precisley reverse state of things has occurred. Towards the end of the last century, my maternal grandfather, a Sheffield cutler named George Wostenholm, chose the three letters I.X.L., as a trade mark for his Cutlery. Its market value at the present moment, protected by Act of Parliment from piracy, as are all marks pertaining to the Cutlers Company, is estimated at not less than £80,000, or over £25,000 a letter!

Exeter.

HARRY HEMS.

We are indebted to Mr. Hems for the blocks from which the illustrations are taken.

EDITOR.

50

e 40   Tuckers Hall

Plate 41   Milk Street (c1930)

Milk Street situated at the top of Fore Street was destroyed in the last war. One side of the street was formed by the side of the Lower Market
photograph shows that it is Christmas. Mistletoe is being sold from the stalls and the windows are decorated. In a small square off this street stoo
obelisk which marked the site of an ancient conduit. The obelisk still stood but was demolished after the war.

Plate 42   Old Houses Fore Street (c1900)

James Crocker, an eminent architect described these two houses as being the "finest examples of their type in the area" in 1886. The first house
said to have been built in the reign of James 1st and the second property constructed during the reign of Charles 1st. Both properties were to bec
one of Exeter's most famous public houses — The Chevalier Inn.

52

53

Plate 43   Equestrian Statue on "The Chevalier Inn"

The Chevalier Inn took its name from a statue which stood high up on its gable. This piece of pottery took the form of a rider on horse back. It was said that these ridge tiles indicated a safe haven for Prince Charles on his route west after the Battle of Worcester. It has also been suggested that such figures denote a place of entertainment, or a Cavaliers House during the Civil Wars. It is indicated that the building was not a place that would welcome the opposition. Such ridge tiles are not common but other examples are found in Totnes. It is possible that the sample shown was not the original.

Plate 44   **The Chevalier Inn (c1930)**

This record shows the Chevalier Inn before its destruction. Its statue is clearly seen on the right hand side ridge. In earlier photographs the building appears without its ridge tile. Could it be that the tile was manufactured to suit the needs of the proprietors? The interior of the building was exceedingly pleasant having fine decorated ceilings on its upper floors.

LLOYD'S CIGARETTE FACTORY

Situated in No. 76 and 77 Fore Street was the Cigarette factory of H. C. Lloyd, whose history stretched from 1784 to the early 1920's. The factory produced cigarettes, cigars, tobacco and snuff. The various products were marketed with some delightful brand names. Cigarettes for instance were called Tipsy Loo, Silver Fir, Lid Lals, Tinners Pipe Tobaccos, Prince Llewelyn Tre, Pol, and Pen 100 A1 at Lloyds.

Although this Company has fallen into obscurity, there is still something which retains its

memory and that is the cigarette cards issued by Messrs. Lloyds. The factory employed a large number of women some of whom were duly photographed and shown on these cards. There were also other subjects chosen, such as famous Generals etc. The eventual closure of the factory was said to be due to the sending of free tobacco to the troops in France during the 1914–18 war. Later, it was taken over by Woolworths and then Exeter Corporation Electricity showrooms until it was blitzed in 1941.

Plate 45   Lloyd's cigarette factory

Plate 46   Statue of St Peter — High Street corner

At this spot the roads of High Street, South Street, North Street and Fore Street meet. In the past it was known as "St Peter's Corner". It obtained [its] name from a significant statue that stood overlooking this junction from a lofty position on the corner of High Street and North Street. Over [the] centuries the statue of St Peter who stands on a pagan image had been gradually placed in higher positions until finally he rested in a special alc[ove] where until recently he remained, as shown in the above photograph. Nobody knows the origin of this rare work which now rests in Exeter's Museu[m]. A poem was created for this unique work which said "When he hears the clock strike four, thumbs a leaf and turns it o'er and then reads on". Thi[s] course refers to the reading of the bible. An Exeter character, "Artful Thomas" would stand looking up at St Peter and generally caused interest in [the] Saint. Convincing people that the statue would "turn its pages o'er" and gathering a large group looking intently upwards he would quietly move aw[ay] leaving them all looking heavenwards!

Plate 47   St Peters Corner   (c1890)

Plate 48   The Guildhall and High Street showing Allhallows Church (c1880)

Following the High Street up from the Guildhall one can see a small building which was on the corner of Goldsmith Street. This was the tiny church Allhallows. It was demolished in 1906. The church which was at one time actually integrated into another building was removed to open up the acc to Goldsmith Street. Again this was to allow greater vehicular access, one of the reasons for the loss of many of Exeter's historic buildings. The adjac buildings, numbers 206 and 207 High Street, at this time "Knapmans the Drapers" were demolished in recent times and reconstructed in concrete. the layman no change would be detected.

Plate 49 **Exeter High Street from Guildhall upwards (c1880)**

EXETER GUILDHALL

Another civic treasure dating back to before the 12th century, Exeter's Guildhall stands prominent in the centre of High Street. It is said the Guildhall is the oldest civic building in the Country.

The present structure was rebuilt in 1330 and the hall re-roofed in 1466. Walking into the fine building you pass through a studded door of solid oak made in 1593. For many years the Guildhall was used as an Assize Court.

Naturally, the Guildhall has been the centre of all civic events presided over by the Mayor in Office, Paintings of some of these distinguished gentlemen hang in the Guildhall Chambers. Within the ancient building lies the City regalia, a priceless treasure, of great antiquity.

Under the portico of the Guildhall the stocks were sited. Drunkards were frequently locked in them and left to sober up! Fortunately this has now been discontinued. It is interesting to note that underneath the portico and still fixed in the ceiling is large hook. This was used to suspend the public scales for the weighing of meat. The pork Butchers shambles covered this part of High Street from Goldsmith Street to Broadgate. The meat was weighed by one of the Guildhall Mace Bearers. Also, goods were deposited in the open reception area of the Guildhall, which is now the Guildhall office.

Plate 50   **The Guildhall (c18**

Plate 51   **The Guildhall and High Street (c1870)**

A knife grinder on the left of the photograph completes an excellent record of Exeter at this period. The Turks Head Pub still had its original front feature of Exeter was its shop blinds. Poles were inserted into holes in the kerb stones to support them. These can still be found today.

Plate 52   **Decorated electric trams at the Guildhall 1905**

Guildhall has been the focal point for many important events but perhaps this was one of the most popular. On April 4th 1905 a cavalcade of
orated trams arrived at the Guildhall for the opening day of Exeter's Electric Tramway. The Mayor, C Perry, addressed citizens from the upper deck.
e the lone spectator on the building adjacent to the Guildhall.

Plate 53   The City Regalia

The City Regalia consists of four Maces, two Swords of State, a Cap of Maintenance, a Mayor's chain and Badge, a Sheriff's Chain and Badge, four Chains for the Sargeants at Mace, a Loving Cup and a Salver.

The oldest sword was given to the City in 1470 by Edward IV with the other sword and Cap of Maintenance given in 1497 by Henry VII. The swords are said to be the only existing examples from early Monarchs.

Plate 54   Interior of the Guildhall (Shown as a Court)

Plate 55   The Vicars Choral South Street

Opposite the West Front of Exeter Cathedral is a small lane which connects with South Street. At the South Street end is a ruin which previously wa[s] ancient Hall. It is shown above. The Hall was blitzed in 1942. In the 14th century the whole of the lane was converted into a community for pri[est] There was the Hall, Kitchen and houses integrated into the complex. The community buildings were to be removed in sections over the centuries above all the Hall was regarded as one of Exeter's historical treasures.

Plate 56   Aerial view of the Cathedral

arly seen in front of the Cathedral is St Mary Major Church which was demolished in 1971. In front of it to the right and fitting into the south street mises can be seen the roof of the Vicars Choral. Note the narrowness of South Street at this time.

EXETER CATHEDRAL

The Cathedral of St Peter has dominated the life of Exeter for nearly 1000 years. Its very style and architecture reflects upon the changes that have taken place within our society during that time. From a photographic viewpoint the Cathedral has changed little since the concept of photography came into being. Perhaps the most significant aspect that one can see with early photographic records is the physical state of the building. It is often seen in a blackened state, not at all like it is seen today. The building has been subject to restoration for many years and it is apparent just how much has been done when one makes direct comparisons.

The aerial views in this book will show the splendid Norman Towers and the magnificent 300 foot long roof stretching between those towers. The photograph opposite shows the Cathedral West Front illuminated for the Octocentenary.

The Cathedral is shown here unscathed but in 1942 a direct hit destroyed St James Chapel. The windows of the great building had been boarded up to protect them. These boards still stayed up for some time after the war.

The Cathedral Bells have rung out over the City for centuries but every now and again some restoration is necessary to keep them in good order. In 1902 some of the bells were recast and as one of the photographs shows created a great deal of interest from local residents. In the South Tower there are twelve bells. The tenor Bell weighs 72 cwt and is called "The Grandisson", after the Bishop from whom it was a gift. In the North Tower there is one bell called "Great Peter" which weighs 125 cwt and dated 1484.

Today the Cathedral stands as proud as ever dominating the City centre, however the City around it has changed in a remarkable way in the last 15 years.

Plate 57   **The Cathedral West Front illuminated**

Plate 58   Recasting of Cathedral bell 1902

After recasting, one of the Cathedral Bells is subject to inspection by some local residents. The children are fascinated and actually tap the bell to ch
its tonal quality! The lady on the left appears to be in a "delicate" state and awaiting the arrival of a new Exonian! The bells were rehung in readiness
the Coronation of Edward VII in 1902.

Plate 59   **Aerial view of the Cathedral and Bedford Circus (c1930)**

THE CATHEDRAL CLOSE

Originally the Cathedral Close was the burial ground for the whole of Exeter. It was not until 1637 that the practice of burying people in The Close changed. After this date Bartholomew Yard was used for the purpose. The buildings around The Close have been used primarily for ecclesiastical purposes housing priests, Bishops and other persons connected with the church. At one time the area was enclosed due to the murder of a member of the church at Broadgate. Seven gates gave access into the Close. Unfortunately none of these gates exist today. Before 1942 the Cathedral Close would have had more traffic than it does today as a road went right in front of the West Front. Parking was allowed. Within The Close were a number of fine mature English Elm Trees, giving the area a very shaded appearance in summer. Tourism was very limited and certainly did not attract the numbers of people we see today.

Traditionally Exeter's Cathedral Close has attracted some eminent businesses who have always sought the prestige of premises in this historical area.

In the last century one of the most well known businesses was that of "Worth & Co" who undertook business from "Mols Coffee House". The company specialised in picture framing, restoration and the selling of paintings, etchings, engravings and postcards. "Worths" produced their own postcards and some excellent Guide Books to the City.

"Wippell & Co" had premises at 23 Cathedral Yard and specialised in Church and House furnishings. They were also outfitters supplying superb clothing with gold and silver embroidery for church purposes. This company still operates in Exeter but in St Thomas. The famous name of "Veitch" was seen at number 17. These famous horticulturalists and seedsmen have a long history and were involved in the first hybridisation of Orchids. They are world famous as orchid collectors and growers. Today their premises is part of "The Well House" Public House. Exeter's finest library and resource on the City and West Country can still be found in "The Devon and Exeter Institution" a wonderful private library housed in what was the Town House of the Courtenay family at 7 The Close. For many years The Close was encircled by ornate iron railings. These were to be removed as part of the war effort. Previously a simple wooden rail with posts were in position. Today it is a short wall that people sit on to gaze at one of England's treasures — The Cathedral Close.

Plate 60   St Martins Church and "Mols Coffee House" (c1890)

 famous and picturesque part of the Cathedral Close shows St Martins Church, Mol's Coffee House and adjacent shops.
 St Martins Church has a very ancient history and dates back to 1065. The shop next door, the most delightful in Exeter, is Mol's Coffee House.
 and 1590 this was owned by an Italian, a certain Mr. Mol, who prospered by offering his establishment for refreshments. It was here that Military
 Naval gentlemen met to discuss the battle against the Spanish Armada.
 In the room on the first floor the walls are panelled in oak and contain 46 coats of arms on small shields approximately 6 inches square. During the
 od shown Mol's Coffee house was occupied by Worth & Co. frame makers, picture cleaners and restorers. This company produced some delightful
 k and helped record the City with their etchings and postcards.

Plate 61   The Globe Hotel, Cathedral Yard

Opposite the West Front of Exeter Cathedral and in the corner of The Cathedral Yard stood one of Exeter's premier hotels — "The Globe". The ori
of the building are a little obscure but it is suggested that it started its life around the mid 17th century but had over the years been extended
changed. It was one of the City's coaching inns and it was possible to walk right through the Hotel and out into South Street. To the left can be se
narrow entrance called "Little stile" which also gave access to the street. The whole of the Hotel was gutted in 1942 and the rem
demolished.

Plate 62   Aerial view towards Queen Street (probably from St Mary majors spire)

king from the Cathedral Close towards Queen Street one can easily see the fine line of façades that once graced the elegant Queen Street. The
olition of these buildings proved to be a controversial move, especially as the new structure was to be totally unsuitable for the site on which it was
ted. Today the site is occupied by 'C & A'.

ROYAL CLARENCE HOTEL

Of all the hotels in Exeter the Royal Clarence in the Cathedral Close is probably the best known. Its central situation overlooks the Cathedral Green. This fine building was erected in 1769 when the first landlord was a Frenchman Peter Berlon — hence the name hotel, derived from the French 'hote'. In the early days it was always referred to as "The Hotel" in the churchyard and was then the first hotel in England.

In 1806 Jenkins History of Exeter contained the following recommendation. "The only house, worthy of notice in its parish is, The Hotel, a large commodious Inn, with elegant apartments and Hotel accommodation for people of the first quality, with a large assembly room in which the assize balls, concerts and assemblies of the most distinguished persons of City and County take place, in the front is a neat coffee room. The situation of "The Hotel" is very pleasant as it opens to the parade and commands a noble view of the Cathedral". In 1815 a meeting was held in the Clarence to discuss the lighting of Exeter by gas. It was to be the first place in the County to receive gas for lighting.

One of the most famous people to visit the Clarence was Horatio Nelson in 1801. He was made an Honorary Freeman of the City and after a grand reception at the Guildhall returned to the "The Hotel".

Having a long history "The Hotel" boasted a fine collection of antiques. Unfortunately, I understand that many of the most valuable and interesting disappeared after changes of ownership. The collection is somewhat smaller today, but not so many years ago 468 pieces were listed.

Plate 63   **The Royal Clarence Hotel**

Plate 64   Catherine Street (c1890)

This early photograph of Catherine Street is probably dated from around 1890. At this time the street contained a variety of smaller intere[s]t properties including the "Swan Inn" shown on the left. Further up the street is an arch way probably stone that obviously led into a passage and m[...] a courtyard. The Devon Cycle works is shown on the right.

Plate 65 (opposite)   Catherine Street (c1910)

At this time there appears to be a distinct improvement in this street and as can be seen it had retained a great deal of character. It was most unfortu[nate] that one of our more pleasant back streets was to lose so many of its buildings due to demolition and the blitz of 1942.

Plate 66   The Exeter Bank (c1910)

Opened in 1769 the Exeter Bank had a prominent position in the City and belonged to the builder of The Royal Clarence Hotel James Mackwe
Praed. In 1902 the bank amalgamated and afterwards "Dellers" took over the building as a café. At a later date it was to become part of the Ro
Clarence Hotel. For a period bank notes from the old business were displayed on the walls of the Hotel.

Plate 67   Hinton and Lake, Numbers 41 and 42, High Street

ginally two houses, these premises have for the most part been more familiar to many Exonians as "Hinton & Lake" Dispensing emists. The company was the most prominent shop for photographic apparatus. Dating from around 1564 the premises today has been rbished to a high standard and is operating under the name of Laura Ashley.

Plate 68   **High Street below Queen Street (c1920)**

Plate 69   Traffic jam in High Street outside Colsons (c1930)

s interesting record shows busy Exeter bustling with people and traffic outside of one of the City's most famous shops "Colsons" (today Dingles).
ay we are far more conscious of traffic and the effect on our environment but perhaps in these days there was still some novelty factor. These
icles today would be collectors items.

Plate 70 Queen Street (c1910)

As from 1833 a decision was made to create a major new road and to build a covered market to get over the problem of congested street markets. new street was to be called "Queen Street" in 1838, the year of Queen Victoria's Coronation. Old Queen Street boasted fine façades on either side could have been classified as a grand street and although in latter years substantial portions were to be lost it still retains its Victorian grande

Plate 71 **The Higher Market and Queen Street (c1910)**

Higher Market was opened in 1838 and closed in 1962. It was a fascinating place to visit where fishmongers, butchers, grocers and other businesses
d their trade. Many people would come into Exeter from the country to sell their wares at the market. The road coming from the north being the
st popular. The structure was retained as part of the new "Golden Heart" project and although it has been retained has lost much of its former
rm by being developed internally.

Plate 72   **The Higher Market, Queen Street**

Plate 73   The Public Information Bureau, Corner of Paul Street

is curious building stood on the edge of Paul Street and Queen Street. It replaced the "Museum Hotel" which had earlier been demolished to allow
opening up of Paul Street. The new structure was to be used as a Public Information Office. It was run independently for the benefit of residents and
itors. Eventually the task of keeping the populous informed was taken over by the City Council. The building was to be demolished to allow for the
w development of Paul Street. The old Bus and Coach Station can be seen in Paul Street.

Plate 74   The opening of the Mile
Memorial Clock Tower 1898

This fine structure was opened by Mrs. Miles c
Dix's Field in 1898. It was dedicated to he
husband who was devoted to the welfare c
animals. Mrs. Miles arrived in a carriage pulled b
two magnificent dapple grey horses. They were th
first to drink from the elaborate drinking trough
The Clock Tower was built by Messrs Eastons
Stone Masons, whose premises until recently
stood adjacent to the City Swimming Baths.

Plate 75   The Quadrangle, (c1890)

is structure stood on the site which was to be taken over for the construction of the Miles Memorial Clock Tower. It appeared to serve the
rpose for which it was intended but without the grandeur. At one time the Clock Tower was threatened with demolition as it was classified as a
ffic hazard.

GENERAL SIR REDVERS BULLER, VC, GCB, GCMG

General Redver's Buller was born at Downes, near Crediton in 1839. At the age of 18 he joined the King's Own Rifles and embarked on a magnificent military career. It can be said that he was to become probably the most famous soldier ever to come from the West Country.

A man of great character, strength and precision he was to be renowned in his own lifetime.

The first major battle in which he participated was the Chinese War of 1860. Later he was to move to Canada and fought in the Red River Campaign in 1867 and again in 1873 in the Ashanti war. The year 1878 brought him to South Africa where his most heroic actions were to take place. Great battles in Egypt also saw his presence.

Although he spent most of his life in a military capacity for a short period in his life he returned to Downes, where he pursued farming activities. General Buller succeeded not only on the battlefield but in farming circles. It was a fact that he possessed some of the finest stock in the country. Certainly no one had finer horses for which he had a famous reputation.

To the local folk he was known as the "Squire of Downes".

Redvers Buller died in 1901 and it was decided that a statue should be erected to his memory in both Exeter and Plymouth. A home was also to be opened for wounded soldiers at Crediton. A shilling fund was opened, but got off to a poor start. However, after a large donation was obtained the general response improved. Money came from all parts of the world. On September 6th 1905 his statue was unveiled in Exeter by the Lord Lieutenant of Devon Viscount Ebrington. Today it still stands outside Bury Meadow.

MEDALS PRESENTED TO GENERAL BULLER

CHINA 1860, 2 clasps; CANADA 1866–70, 3 clasps; ASHANTI 1873, 1 clasp; SOUTH AFRICA 1878–9, Victoria Cross; EGYPT 1882, 4 clasps; JUBILEE MEDAL; SOUTH AFRICA 1889–1901, 6 clasps.

Plate 76   **The erection of The Buller Memorial 1905**

Plate 77   The erection of the South Gate for Victoria's Jubilee 1897

Amongst many activities which were organised for the celebration of Queen Victoria's Jubilee in 1897 was the concept of rebuilding the City's ancient Gates. Shown above is the South Gate which straddled South Street just above the "White Hart Hotel". A coach has just passed through the Gate coming into the City. South Street at this time was far narrower than it is today. The old South Gate was removed in 1819.

Plate 78 The erection
of The North Gate 1897 at
the Iron Bridge

THE ANCIENT HOUSE OF "ROSS" HIGH STREET

Plate 79   Numbers 226 and 227 High Street

Dating from around 1890 this photograph shows two of Exeter's finest historical buildings dating from the 17th century. They have been subject to significant restoration and still grace the High Street. The façades only exist as considerable vandalism took place with the whole insides of the buildings being ripped out. It can be said that the frontages are only held as a token of the past and are a classic example of the lack of interest and damage that has been done to the City's buildings in the past. Today it is unlikely that such activities would be allowed. The building number 227 was known more commonly as the premises of "Ross the Tailor" a classical business of its type. Adjacent to it was "The Civet Cat" a local pub. Number 226 was at this time occupied by the publishing and Printing Offices of The "Devon Evening Express" and "Devon Weekly News". Next to it was "A Mashford, Milliner and Hatter".

Plate 80 **The Devon and Somerset Stores High Street (c1900)**

The premises of numbers 245 and 246 High Street were occupied by the well known "Devon and Somerset Stores". They were known for their quality foodstuffs. Here they are recorded holding their annual Xmas Bazaar. The lack of people in the street is the result of the camera taking the photograph at a very slow speed. The images of the people are hardly recorded. A line of cabs stand outside St Lawrence's Church, perhaps waiting for some of the congregation. Behind them is advertised "Wilsons Guildhall Restaurant".

Deller's Café

The Popular Resort for LUNCHEONS Dainty Afternoon Teas and Dinners.

String Orchestra Daily.
VERY MODERATE CHARGES.

Open Daily
from 9 a.m. to 9 p.m.

Bedford St. EXETER,
And at Paignton.

Plate 81   **Dellers Café advert**

Plate 82   Dellers Café, Dining Room

No other building can compete with Dellers Café for evoking memories. It was the most popular haunt where Exonians enjoyed themselves. Situated in Bedford Street with a grand entrance, the café was built partly over a one storey building used by Lloyds bank. This was "The" meeting place for Exonians. It was where the orchestra played, the people danced, grand banquets and Balls were held and people came for their afternoon teas. These premises which were opened in 1916 were tragically lost in the Second World War.

Plate 83   Dellers Café interior

Plate 84   Bedford Circus (c1920)

Formerly on the site of a Dominican Monastery, Bedford Circus, a crescent of houses with a church, was the finest piece of Georgian architecture in City. The central area contained an oval garden with railings around it. Many prominent people had offices in the Circus and at its entrance from H Street stood the statue of Lord Courtenay erected in 1878. The statue is the only remains from Bedford Circus that exists today. Although damaged wartime raids the Circus still had sections standing. Although recommendations were put forward to reconstruct, all the remaining Circus demolished.

Plate 85 **The unveiling of the Courtenay statue 8th October 1880**

Plate 86   The entrance to Dix's Field (c1920)

Dix's Field, started in the early 19th century, was one of Exeter's most exclusive places to live. Flanked by beautiful private houses on each side, its m. feature was a central area of gardens. The vast majority of the Dix's Field was destroyed in the blitz of 1942. A small section has been retained, restor and today has been the instigation for retaining some of the style of its builder Matthew Nosworthy.

Plate 87   The Half Moon Hotel, High Street (c1900)

On the corner of High Street and Bedford Street stood a very large hotel called "The Half Moon Hotel". It was from all accounts a very substantial structure. In 1912 it was demolished and was replaced by a single storey building which was to be occupied by Lloyds Bank. Later Dellers Café was to be incorporated into the site to the side and over the top of Lloyds Bank

Plate 88 **Central High Street showing Commercial Union and Brufords (c1930)**

Opposite Dellers Café in High Street stood some of the most prominent Exeter businesses. Their properties often reflected the importance of their success. On the far left is perhaps the grandest of all the High Street property frontages which was that of the Commercial Union Assurance Co. On top of its façades stood the statue of King Alfred. Although the whole statue survived the war only the bust has been retained. The Goldsmiths and Silversmiths "Brufords" was next door with its magnificent clock of "Old Father Time". Fred Ford Signs was adjacent to "The Devon and Somerset Stores".

Plate 89   **High Street showing St Lawrence's Church (c1930)**

e focal point of this section of High Street was the church of St Lawrence. Above its entrance was the figure of Elizabeth 1st. The vast majority of the
eet was devastated during the blitz of 1942 but although gutted the church still stood. It was later demolished. The statue can still be seen today in the
ices of the Commercial Union in Bedford Street. The Empire Cinema was next door to the church.

Plate 90 **High Street from The London Inn Square showing the Arcade (left)**

Plate 91   The Eastgate Arcade (c1910)

uated just opposite the London Inn was the fashionable East Gate Arcade. It was here that some of Exeter's quality shops could be found. Walking ough the entrance the customer was confronted by a long arcade, at its end was constructed a huge circular stained glass window. The Arcade would en have floral displays. One of Exeter's top photographic studios had premises there "Chandlers" and also "Cummings" the umbrella maker, who l trade in Exeter today. This wonderful classic arcade was tragically lost during the war and although we have undercover shopping in the City today e arcade is still remembered. It was situated at the top of Princesshay running from High Street to Post Office Street.

Plate 92   Poples New London Hotel, London Inn Square (c1870)

This prestigious Hotel was the centre for coaching in Exeter. Around 70 coaches a day left the premises and some 3000 people are estimated to ha been involved directly or indirectly with coaching activities when at its peak. All Mail coaches started here. The coach the "Quicksilver" could achi London in 20 hours. Coaches also used other hotels, The Half Moon, The White Horse, White Lion etc. The coach called "The Defiance" used fo splendid Greys. One Christmas a coach piled high with goods turned over and killed the driver, on another occasion a Baron took the reins a managed to turn the coach over. The Inspector of Mail was a passenger and from that time on no unauthorised person was allowed to dr coaches.

Plate 93 **The interior courtyard The New London Hotel**

Plate 94   **The London Inn Square (c1930)**

Plate 95 **The corner of Paris Street and Sidwell Street (c1925)**

EXETER THEATRE ROYAL

One of the most interesting buildings that existed in Exeter, was the Theatre Royal which had a long and fascinating history. Unfortunately, it has been one of the saddest.

The Theatre played host to some of the greatest entertainers of the stage that had been seen in this country. The best stage shows were seen, World Premiers opened to its floodlights. The history of this building and what it stood for, would alone command a book. Theatres have existed in Waterbeer Street and Bedford Street, where two were built and both destroyed by fire. The last site was the corner of Longbrook Street and New North Road.

Incredibly, even after greater fire precautions fate struck for a third time.

The romantic drama "Romany Rye" opened to a full house on September 5th 1887, a date which stands dominant in Exeter's history.

Around 10.00 p.m., a drop scene fell and was the prelude to a horrific ending to the evening. Seconds later the curtain bulged forward not much notice was taken, once again the curtain bulged and this time someone called "Fire". A panic stricken rush took place, people fell crushing each other as they pressed to the Exit. Women jumped 40 feet from the side balcony into the street, sustaining terrible injuries.

Fire engines rushed to the scene from the Railway, Higher Barracks and Topsham. Adding to the confusion 50 horses were released from Pickfords next door and galloped off in all directions.

By the early hours of the morning the bodies were removed from the Theatre and the exact magnitude of the disaster was then realised. A horrifying total of 186 bodies were recovered. The corpses were laid out in the yard and stables of the London Inn.

At the inquest the blame was laid on bad design and construction of the building, and lack of inspection when completed. After this, Parliament requested a complete review of the fire and safety regulations for all theatres. A result of this review was the introduction of the fire curtain and the Theatre Royal was the first to install one on rebuilding. The safety curtain would be lowered in a prompt 20 seconds. It weighed 4½ tons and took four men to winch it up.

Sadly, the Theatre Royal was demolished in 1962 and with it ended the source of some of the most interesting history of this country's Theatre. Exeter's Theatre today is no longer situated in the city centre, but housed in the University grounds. Now, an insurance building stands on the site of the old Theatre Royal.

Plate 96   **The Theatre Royal, Bedford Street after the fire 1885**

Plate 97   **The gutted Theatre Royal 1887**

Plate 98   **Inspection of the Theatre Royal — Taken from The New London Hotel 1887**

Plate 99 **Aerial view of The London Inn Square (c1930)**

Plate 100   **The Theatre Royal, Longbrook Street**

Plate 101　The Police Station, Waterbeer Street

Built in 1887 the Police Station was conveniently situated to walk prisoners across the road and into the Guildhall for trial. An unusual feature of the building was its section of Roman pavement in the vestibule. Part was original and a section replicated to cover the whole of a floor area. This feature which was later removed with the demolition of the building was to be destroyed in 1972 due to a lack of knowledge by those in charge of safety at the time.

Plate 102   Northernhay Gardens (c1900)

These delightful gardens which offer superb views over the Devon countryside are the oldest public gardens in the country. They have always been a favourite with Exonians. One of the features of the gardens was its magnificent avenue of English Elms. These can be seen standing at the edge of the park. Due to Dutch Elm Disease all these trees had to be removed. The gardens contain numerous statues of interest. These gardens still offer peace and tranquility to Exeter's residents.

Plate 103   Maude's Motor Mart, Paris Street (c1920)

Prewar Paris Street was far narrower than it is today and with post war changes the actual road width was altered. Besides a cinema there were a number of small shops and businesses. These wonderful vehicles were on sale from "Maude's Motor Mart". At a cost of £162 10s you must have had an absolute bargain!

Plate 104   Tram in Paris Street near the Tram Depot

Old Paris Street used to continue until it reached the Triangle at Newtown. This photograph is taken at the point where the street would run down hill just opposite the Tram Depot, later to become the Bus Depot. The Depot was demolished and replaced by flats.

THE TRAMWAYS IN EXETER

The trams of Exeter date back to around the year 1881. For over 20 years they were horse drawn. The tracks for the trams were laid from Livery Dole to St Davids via New North Road; Paris Street to Blackboy Road.

Great difficulties occurred with St Davids Hill, as apparently the horses used were not of the best calibre. The problem of maintenance of road surfaces was a major factor that eventually led to the takeover by the city council, and the private company which was running the trams dissolved.

The introduction of trams in Exeter caused great consternation and the public didn't respond at all well to the idea of having iron tracks placed down through High Street.

The council however, decided the trams were to become electrified. The Mayor and other notables visited a number of countries which were using trams, in order to decide the best system for Exeter.

A new generating station was built on the side of the basin to supply the trams with essential power. The new trams started in 1905.

The route for the trams was as follows:

Livery Dole to Eastgate, thence High Street, Queen Street to St Davids. Cemetery Road to Blackboy Road and Sidwell Street to Eastgate. A route was also placed from Eastgate to Dunsford Gardens. Naturally, this route went over the new Exe Bridge. To accommodate this new track various obstructions were removed in St Thomas.

The completed track was 4.95 miles. The gauge was 3 feet 6 inches.

The system boasted 12 tram cars, which were double deckers and held 54 persons. Each car weighed 8½ tons, was 26 foot long and was powered by two 25 horse power motors. Besides the traditional handbrake the Newall magnetic track brake was also fitted.

Costing of the Tramways

New track and wooden paving, £34,000; Overhead equipment, £4,700; Feed cables, £3,000; Tramcars, £7,000; Shed, £5,700; Generating plant, £4,000. Total cost £584,000.

The Mayor Mr. C Perry drove the first tram powered by electricity, and he also drove the last in 1931. The tram shed was then used as the bus depot until recently and demolished in 1976.

Plate 105   Laying of tram lines at High Street and Queen Street (c1905)

Plate 106   **Horse drawn tram in Heavitree Road**

Plate 107 **Electric tram**

Plate 108 **The first electric tram with Mayor C Perry driving 1905**

Plate 109   **The last electric tram at Heavitree Road with Mayor C Perry driving 19th August 1931**

Plate 110   Horse trams in Sidwell Street outside the White Lion Hotel.
These may have been the last trams to be used

Plate 111 **Sidwell Street in its heyday (c1920)**

131

Plate 112   Mr. Mondy, Master Butcher of Sidwell Street

Mr. Mondy was a Master Butcher whose premises were at Red Lion Court, Sidwell Street. At Christmas it was his tradition to hang an enormou quantity of carcases on the outside of his shop. For this special event he undertook an activity called "Ferning". Each carcase would be carefully carvee with a fern on each flank.

Plate 113   The meeting of Sidwell Street, Old Tiverton Road and Blackboy Road (c1930)

n the foreground can be seen a police box. This was used by the duty policeman of the day. In front of it is a drinking trough for horses, donated by Arthur Kempe. This has been resited at the bottom of Blackboy Road. On the left can be seen a man with a "Cathedral Dairy" handcart. This business could be found opposite the London Inn Square.

St. Sidwells, Exeter.

Plate 114   The Horse Trough, St Sidwells

Situated at the junction of these three roads can be found the almshouses which were originally designed for eight poor people. There is a tiny chapel on this site which completes a charming group of buildings. It is said that originally a hermit lived on this site before it was changed into almshouses in 1561. Called "St Annes Almshouses" the saint was celebrated on July 26th. The almshouses are seen without the brick porch that stands at the entrance today. A new group of houses were also built on the site.

Plate 115　　**Coach leaving Exeter through the Mount Pleasant Toll Gate**

ACKNOWLEDGEMENTS

I should like to thank the many people in Exeter who have taken an interest in The Isca Collection and my thanks to them for supporting the publications I have been involved with over the years.

The many people who have come forward with photographs and information on "Old Exeter" are too numerous to mention but it is appropriate that due thanks are paid to them.

This book is dedicated to
Mr. and Mrs. Thomas